Impressum
Verlag: BABADADA GmbH, Nedderfeld 112 , 22529 Hamburg
Geschäftsführer / Verlagsleitung: Harald Hof
Druck: Books on Demand GmbH, In de Tarpen 42, 22848 Norderstedt

Imprint
Publisher: BABADADA GmbH, Nedderfeld 112 , 22529 Hamburg, Germany
Managing Director / Publishing direction: Harald Hof
Print: Books on Demand GmbH, In de Tarpen 42, 22848 Norderstedt

학교
school

나누다
divide

`186/2`

칠판
board

교실
classroom

학교 운동장
school yard

교사
teacher

종이
paper

펜
pen

쓰다
write

책상
desk

자
ruler

책
book

학생
pupil

책가방
satchel

필통
pencil case

연필
pencil

연필깎이
pencil sharpener

지우개
rubber

스케치북
drawing pad

그림
drawing

붓
paintbrush

그림물감 통
paint box

가위
scissors

풀
glue

연습장
exercise book

숙제
homework

12

숫자
number

2+2

더하다
add

5-2

빼다
subtract

2×2

곱하다
multiply

계산하다
calculate

A

글자
letter

ABCDEFG
HIJKLMN
OPQRSTU
VWXYZ

알파벳
alphabet

hello

낱말
word

텍스트

text

읽다

read

분필

chalk

수업시간

lesson

출석부

register

시험

examination

증명서

certificate

교복

school uniform

교육

education

백과사전

encyclopedia

대학교

university

현미경

microscope

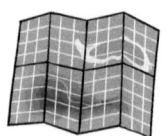

지도

map

휴지통

waste-paper basket

여행

travel

Grand
호텔
hotel
호스텔
hostel
ROOMS
EXCHANGE
환전소
currency exchange office
여행가방
suitcase
자동차
car

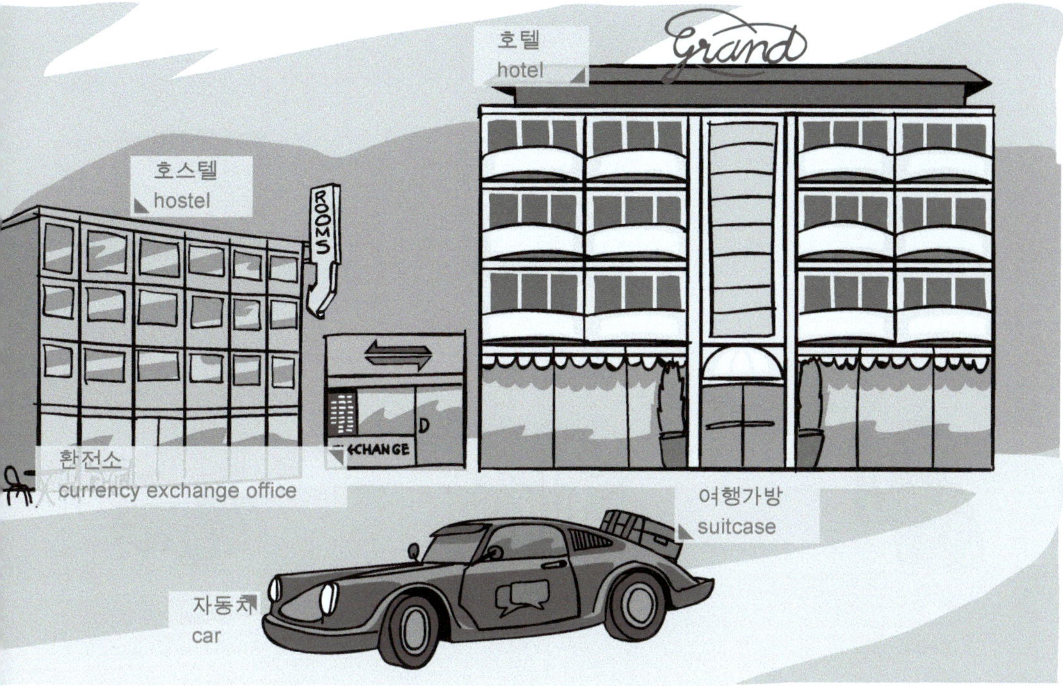

언어

language

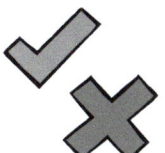

예 / 아니오

yes / no

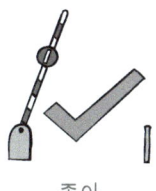

좋아

Okay

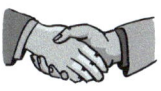

안녕

hello

번역가

translator

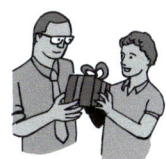

고마워, 고마워요

Thank you

... 얼마입니까?

how much is...?

나는 이해하지 못합니다

I don´t get it

문제

problem

안녕하세요!

Good evening!

안녕하세요!

Good morning!

잘자요!

Good night!

또 만나요

goodbye

방향

direction

수하물

luggage

가방

bag

배낭

backpack

손님

guest

방

room

침낭

sleeping bag

텐트

tent

여행 안내

tourist information

해변

beach

신용카드

credit card

아침식사

breakfast

점심식사

lunch

저녁식사

dinner

승차권

Ticket

승강기

elevator

우표

stamp

경계

border

세관

customs

대사관

embassy

비자

visa

여권

passport

여행 - travel

운반

transport

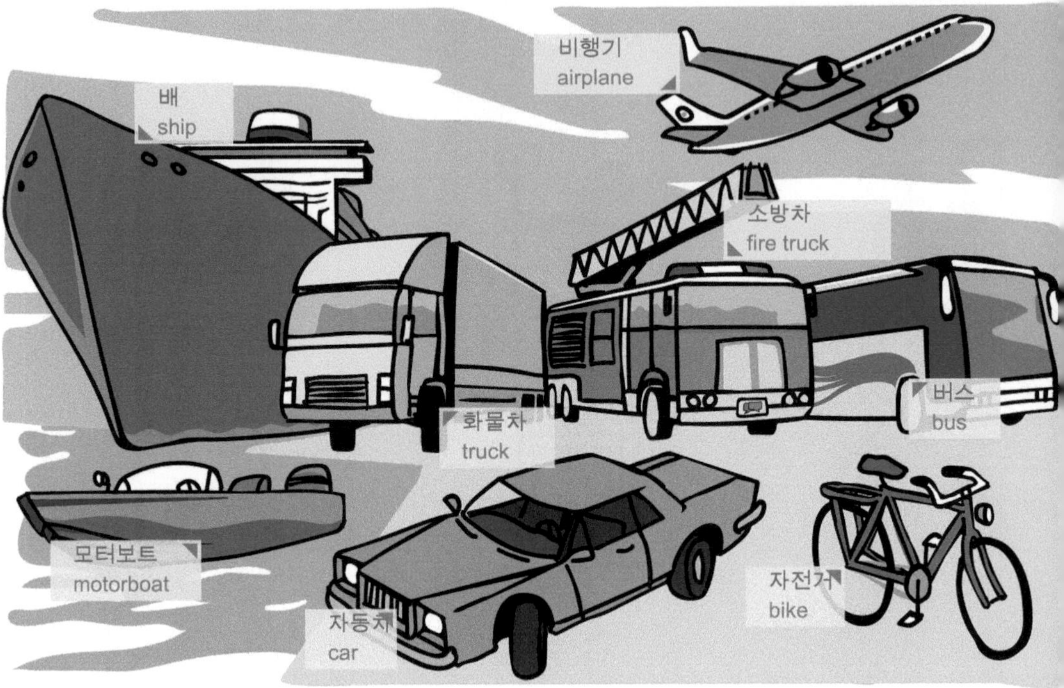

비행기
airplane
배
ship
소방차
fire truck
버스
bus
화물차
truck
모터보트
motorboat
자전거
bike
자동차
car

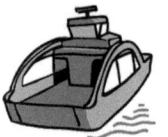

페리

ferry

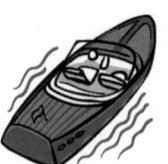

보트

boat

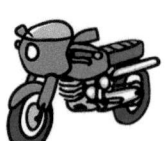

오토바이

motorbike

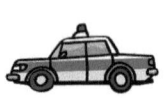

경찰차

police car

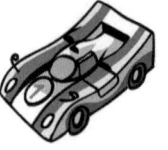

경주차

racing car

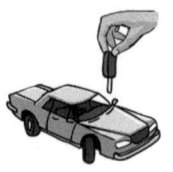

렌트카

rental car

카셰어링

car sharing

견인차

tow truck

쓰레기차

garbage truck

모터

engine

연료

fuel

주유소

fuel station

교통 표지

traffic sign

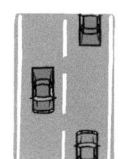

교통

traffic

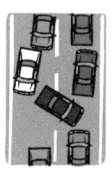

교통 정체

traffic jam

주차장

parking lot

기차역

train station

트랙터

tracks

기차

train

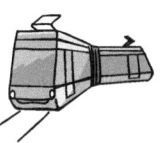

전차

tram

객차

wagon

헬리콥터

helicopter

공항

airport

타워

tower

승객

passenger

컨테이너

container

상자

carton

카트

cart

바구니

basket

출발하다 / 도착하다

take off / land

도시

city

마을

village

도심

city center

집

house

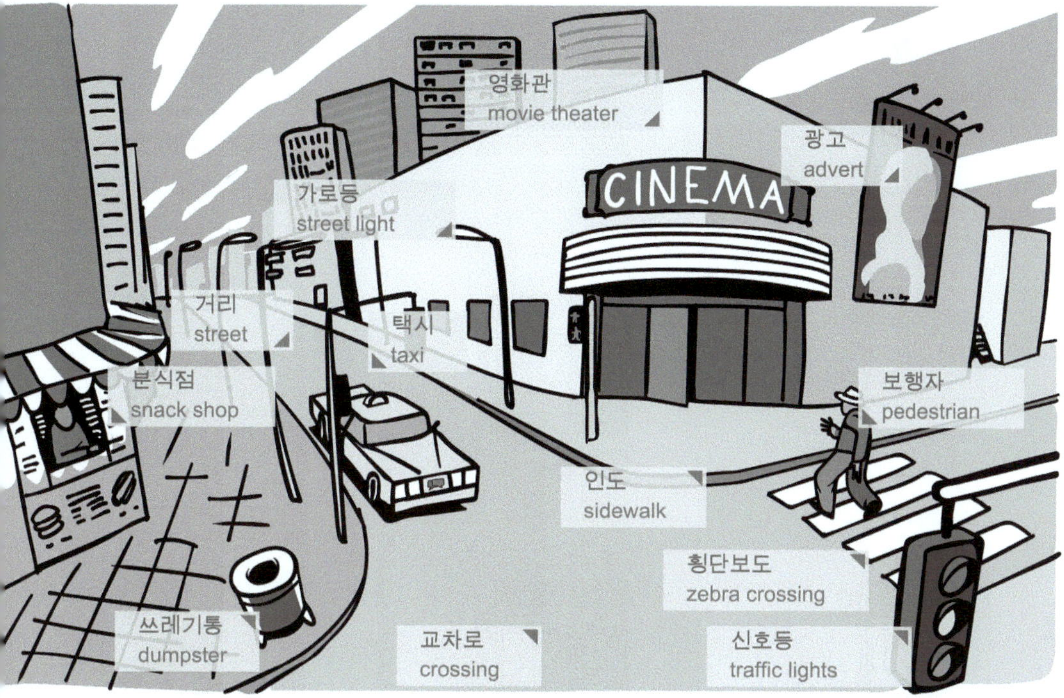

영화관
movie theater
광고
advert
CINEMA
가로등
street light
거리
street
택시
taxi
분식점
snack shop
보행자
pedestrian
인도
sidewalk
횡단보도
zebra crossing
쓰레기통
dumpster
교차로
crossing
신호등
traffic lights

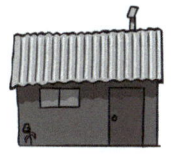

오두막

hut

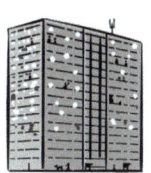

주택

apartment

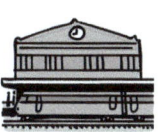

기차역

train station

시청

city hall

MUSEUM

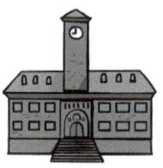

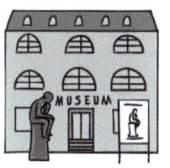

박물관

museum

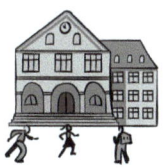

학교

school

대학교
university

은행
bank

병원
hospital

호텔
hotel

약국
pharmacy

사무실
office

서점
book shop

상점
shop

꽃가게
flower shop

수퍼마켓
supermarket

시장
market

백화점
department store

생선가게
fishmonger's shop

쇼핑 센터
mall

항구
harbor

공원

park

벤치

bench

다리

bridge

계단

stairs

지하철

subway

터널

tunnel

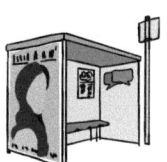

버스 정류장

bus stop

바

bar

레스토랑

restaurant

우체통

postbox

도로 표지판

street sign

주차료 징수기

parking meter

동물원

zoo

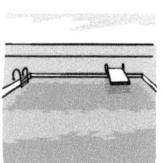

수영장

swimming pool

모스크 사원

mosque

농장

farm

환경오염

pollution

공동묘지

cemetery

교회

church

놀이터

playground

절

temple

풍경

landscape

잎
leaf

이정표
signpost

길
path

초원
meadow

돌
stone

나무
tree

도보여행자
hiker

강
river

잔디
grass

꽃
flower

계곡
valley

산
hill

호수
lake

숲
forest

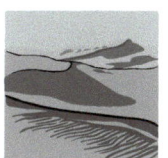

사막
desert

화산
volcano

성
castle

무지개
rainbow

버섯
mushroom

야자나무
palm tree

모기
mosquito

파리
fly

개미
ant

벌
bee

거미
spider

딱정벌레

beetle

개구리

frog

다람쥐

squirrel

고슴도치

hedgehog

토끼

hare

부엉이

owl

새

bird

백조

swan

맷돼지

boar

사슴

deer

순록

moose

댐

dam

풍력 터빈

wind turbine

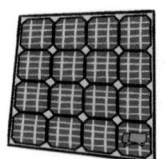

태양광 전지판

solar panel

기후

climate

레스토랑
restaurant

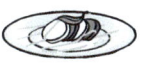

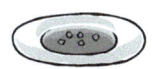

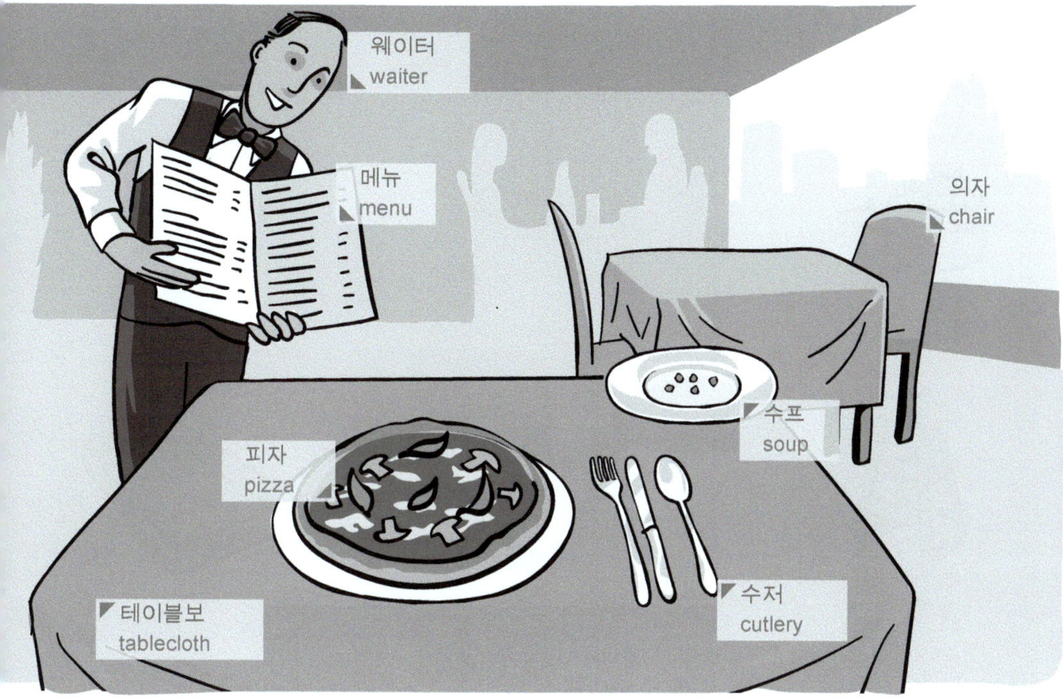
웨이터
waiter
메뉴
menu
의자
chair
수프
soup
피자
pizza
수저
cutlery
테이블보
tablecloth

전채요리

starter

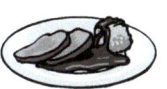

주요리

main course

후식

dessert

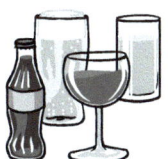

음료수

drinks

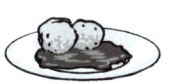

음식

food

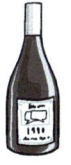

병

bottle

인스턴트 식품

fast food

길거리음식

street food

찻주전자

teapot

설탕통

sugar bowl

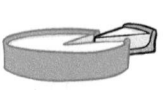

인분

portion

에스프레소 머신

espresso machine

높은 의자

high chair

계산서

bill

쟁반

tray

칼

knife

포크

fork

숟가락

spoon

찻숟가락

teaspoon

냅킨

serviette

유리잔

glass

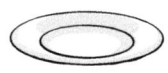

접시

plate

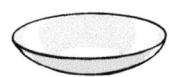

수프 그릇

soup plate

컵 받침

saucer

소스

sauce

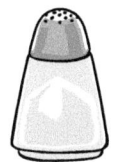

소금통

salt shaker

후추통

pepper mill

식초

vinegar

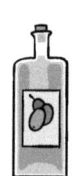

기름

oil

양념

spices

케첩

ketchup

겨자

mustard

마요네즈

mayonnaise

수퍼마켓

supermarket

특가 판매
special offer
FOR
고객
customer
유제품
dairy products
과일
fruit
트롤리
shopping cart

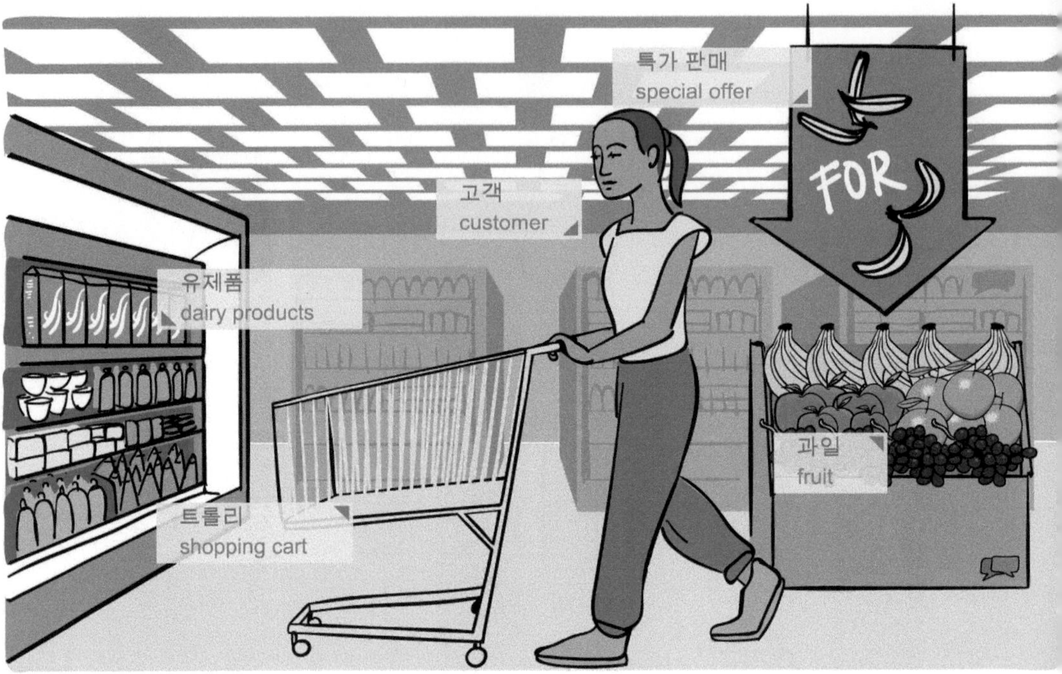

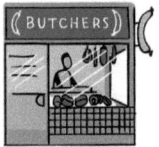

BUTCHERS

정육점

butcher's shop

BAKERY

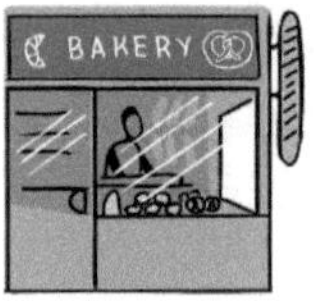

빵집

bakery

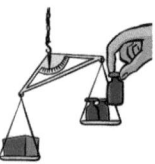

무게가 나가다

weigh

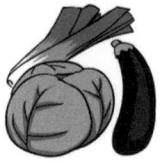

채소

vegetables

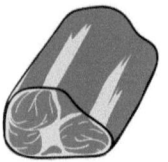

고기

meat

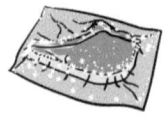

냉동식품

frozen food

냉육

cold cuts

통조림

canned food

가루 세제

detergent

달콤한 간식

candy

가정용품

household products

세척제

cleaning products

판매원

sales representative

계산대

cash register

계산원

cashier

구매목록

shopping list

문 여는 시간

opening hours

지갑

wallet

신용카드

credit card

가방

bag

비닐 봉투

plastic bag

물
water

주스
juice

우유
milk

콜라
coke

와인
wine

맥주
beer

술
alcohol

카카오
cocoa

차고
tea

커피
coffee

에스프레소
espresso

카푸치노
cappuccino

바나나

banana

사과

apple

오렌지

orange

수박

melon

레몬

lemon

당근

carrot

마늘

garlic

대나무

bamboo

양파

onion

버섯

mushroom

견과류

nuts

국수

noodles

스파게티

spaghetti

쌀

rice

샐러드

salad

감자칩

fries

감자튀김

fried potatoes

피자

pizza

햄버거

hamburger

샌드위치

sandwich

커틀렛

escalope

햄

ham

살라미

salami

소시지

sausage

닭

chicken

구이

roast

생선

fish

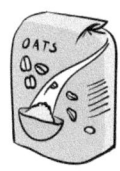

오트밀

porridge oats

뮤슬리

muesli

콘플레이크

cornflakes

밀가루

flour

크루아상

croissant

롤빵

bread roll

빵

bread

토스트

toast

비스킷

cookies

버터

butter

응유

curd

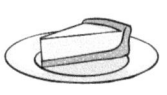

케이크

cake

달걀

egg

계란 후라이

fried egg

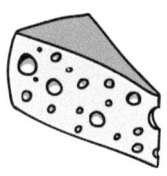

치즈

cheese

아이스크림

ice cream

설탕

sugar

꿀

honey

잼

jelly

누가 크림

nougat cream

카레

curry

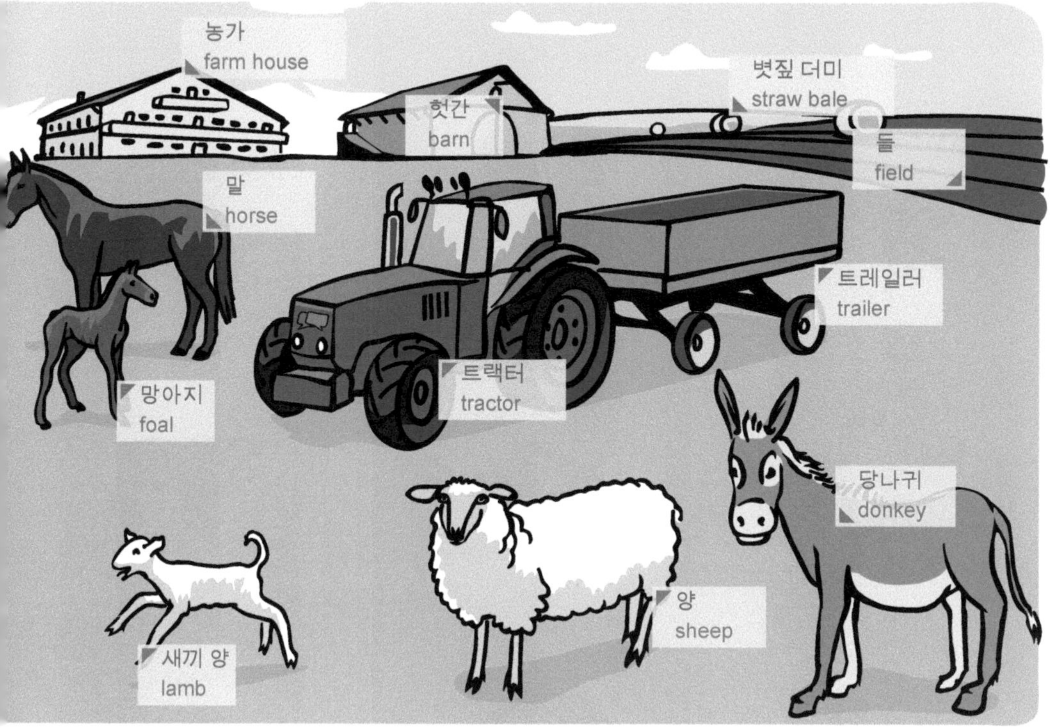

농가
farm house

헛간
barn

볏짚 더미
straw bale

들
field

말
horse

트레일러
trailer

망아지
foal

트랙터
tractor

당나귀
donkey

새끼 양
lamb

양
sheep

염소

goat

암소

cow

송아지

calf

돼지

pig

새끼 돼지

piglet

황소

bull

거위

goose

오리

duck

병아리

chick

암탉

hen

수탉

cockerel

쥐

rat

고양이

cat

생쥐

mouse

황소

ox

개

dog

개집

dog house

정원용 호스

garden hose

물뿌리개

watering can

큰 낫

scythe

쟁기

plow

낫
sickle

괭이
hoe

쇠스랑
pitchfork

도끼
axe

외바퀴 손수레
pushcart

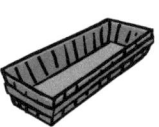

여물통
trough

우유 캔
milk can

부대
sack

울타리
fence

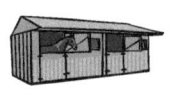

축사
stable

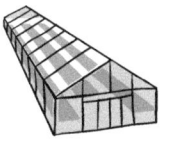

비닐하우스
greenhouse

땅
soil

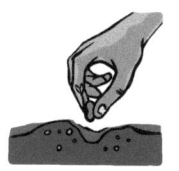

씨앗
seed

거름
fertilizer

콤바인
combine harvester

수확하다

harvest

수확

harvest

참마

yams

밀

wheat

콩

soya

감자

potato

옥수수

corn

유채씨

rapeseed

과일나무

fruit tree

카사바

manioc

곡식

grain

집

house

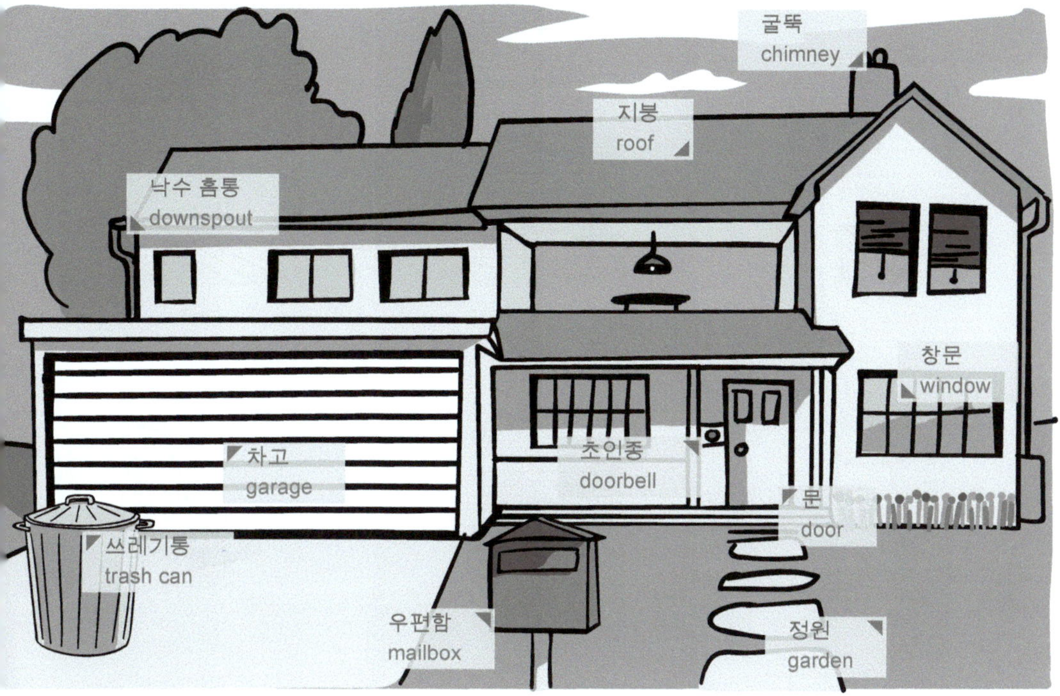

굴뚝
chimney
지붕
roof
낙수 홈통
downspout
창문
window
차고
garage
초인종
doorbell
문
door
쓰레기통
trash can
우편함
mailbox
정원
garden

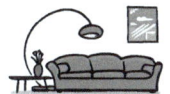

응접실

living room

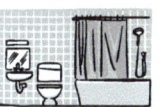

욕실

bathroom

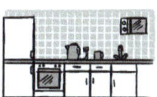

부엌

kitchen

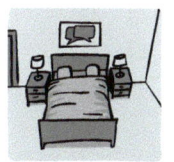

침실

bedroom

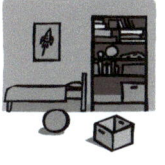

아이들 방

kids room

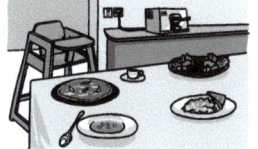

식사실

dining room

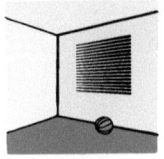

바닥

floor

벽

wall

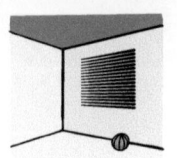

천장

ceiling

지하실

cellar

사우나

sauna

발코니

balcony

테라스

terrace

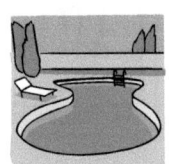

수영장

pool

잔디 깎는 기계

lawn mower

침대 시트

sheet

이불

bedspread

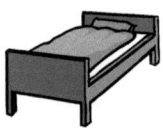

침대

bed

빗자루

broom

양동이

bucket

스위치

switch

응접실

living room

벽지
wallpaper
그림
picture
전등
lamp
선반
shelf
캐비닛
cabinet
텔레비전
television
벽난로
fireplace
꽃
flower
쿠션
cushion
소파
sofa
꽃병
vase
리모컨
remote control

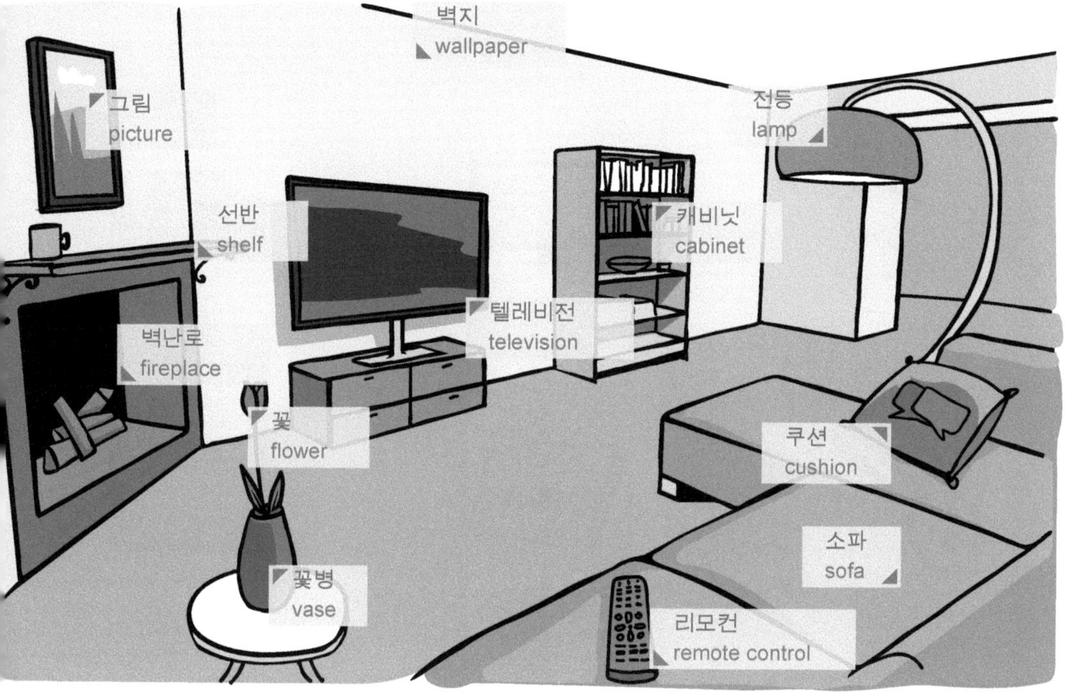

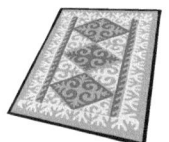

카페트

carpet

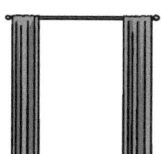

커튼

drape

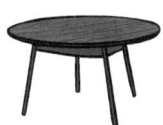

탁자

table

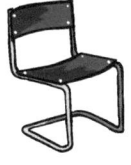

의자

chair

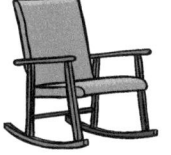

흔들의자

rocking chair

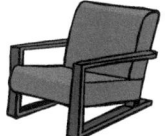

안락의자

armchair

책
....
book

담요
....
blanket

장식
....
decoration

뗄감나무
....
firewood

영화
....
film

하이파이 기기
....
stereo system

열쇠
....
key

신문
....
newspaper

회화
....
painting

포스터
....
poster

라디오
....
radio

노트
....
notebook

진공청소기
....
vacuum cleaner

선인장
....
cactus

초
....
candle

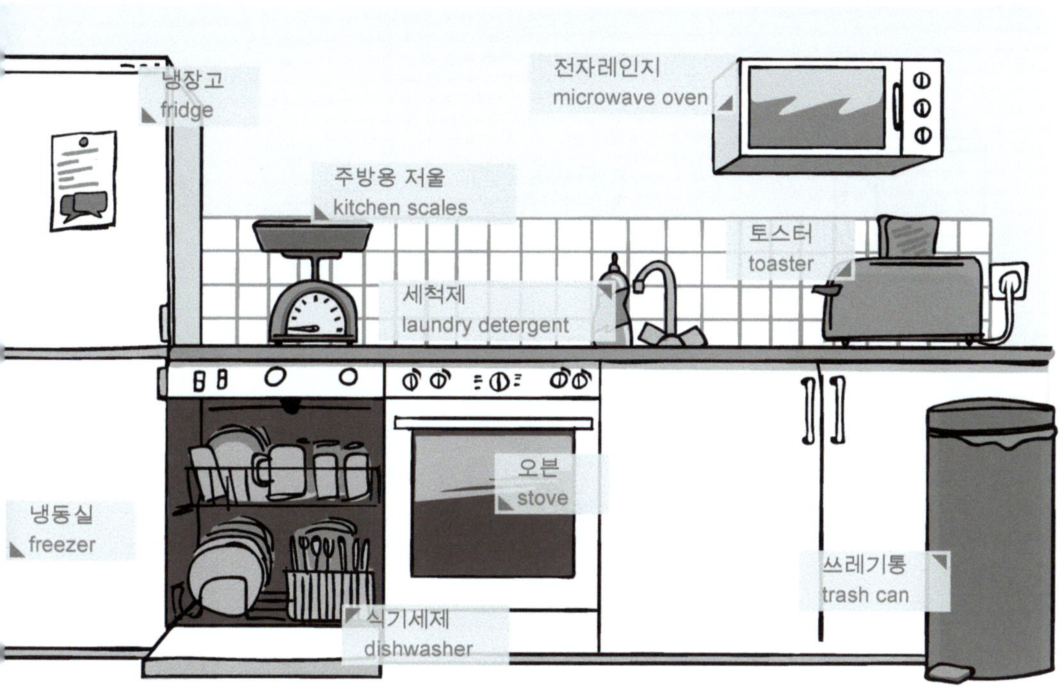

냉장고
fridge

전자레인지
microwave oven

주방용 저울
kitchen scales

세척제
laundry detergent

토스터
toaster

냉동실
freezer

오븐
stove

쓰레기통
trash can

식기세제
dishwasher

쿠커

cooker

냄비

pot

주철 냄비

cast-iron pot

웍 / 카다이 냄비

wok / kadai

프라이팬

pan

주전자

kettle

찜기

steamer

오븐 구이용 쟁반

baking tray

그릇

crockery

머그

mug

양푼이

bowl

젓가락

chopsticks

국자

ladle

주걱

spatula

거품기

whisk

여과기

strainer

체

sieve

강판

grater

절구

mortar

바베큐

barbecue

화덕

fireplace

도마

chopping board

밀방망이

rolling pin

코르크 병따개

corkscrew

캔

can

캔 따개

can opener

냄비 받침

oven cloth

개수대

sink

솔

brush

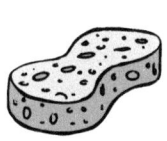

수세미

sponge

블렌더

blender

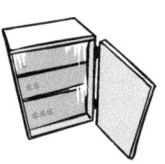

냉동고

deep freezer

젖병

baby bottle

수도꼭지

tap

욕실

bathroom

히터
heating
수건
towel
샤워
shower
샤워 커튼
shower curtain
거품 비누
bubble bath
욕조
bathtub
유리잔
glass
세탁기
washing machine
타일
tiles
수도꼭
지
tap
변기
potty
개수대
sink

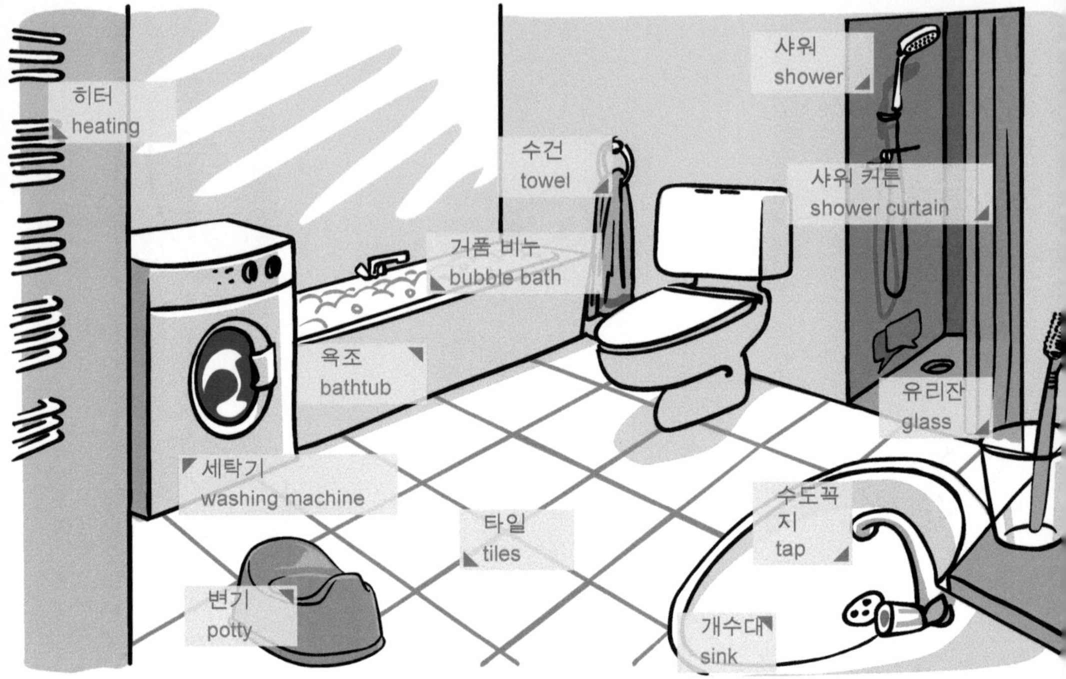

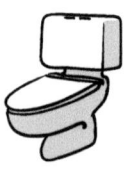

화장실

toilet

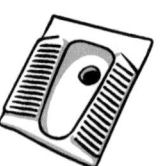

재래식 화장실

squat toilet

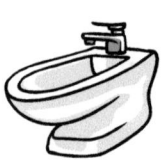

비데

bidet

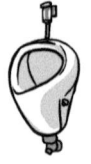

공중 변소

urinal

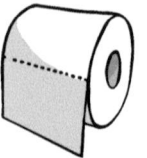

화장지

toilet paper

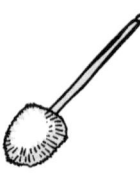

변기솔

toilet brush

치솔

toothbrush

치약

toothpaste

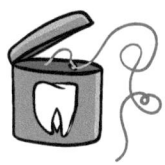

치실

dental floss

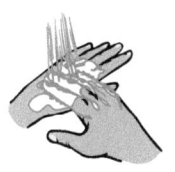

씻다

wash

샤워기

hand shower

질 세척제

douche

대야

basin

등밀이솔

back brush

비누

soap

샤워 젤

shower gel

샴푸

shampoo

물걸레

flannel

배수관

drain

크림

creme

체취 제거제

deodorant

거울

mirror

휴대용 거울

hand mirror

면도기

razor

면도 거품

shaving foam

에프터쉐이브

aftershave

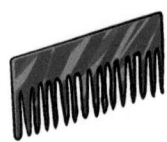

빗

comb

솔

brush

헤어드라이기

hair-dryer

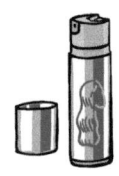

헤어스프레이

hairspray

메이크업

makeup

립스틱

lipstick

손톱깎이

nail varnish

면 솜

cotton wool

손톱

nail scissors

향수

perfume

세면도구 주머니

washbag

스툴

stool

저울

weighing scales

목욕 가운

bathrobe

고무 장갑

rubber gloves

탐폰

tampon

생리대

sanitary towel

화학 화장실

chemical toilet

아이들 방

kids room

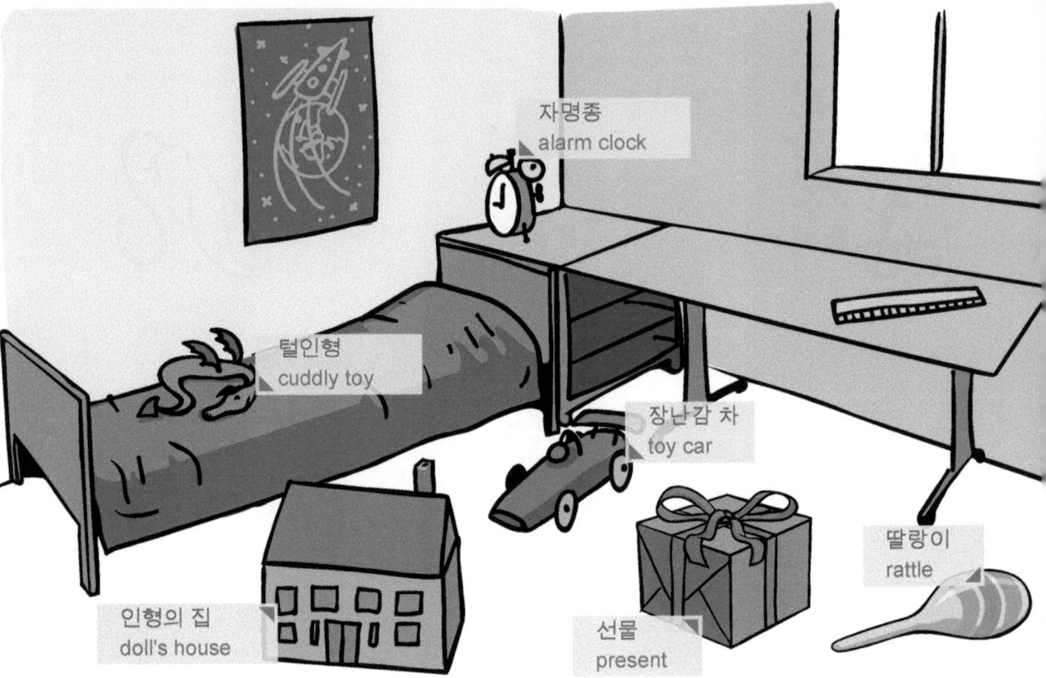

자명종
alarm clock
털인형
cuddly toy
장난감 차
toy car
딸랑이
rattle
인형의 집
doll's house
선물
present

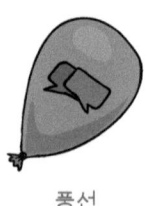

풍선

balloon

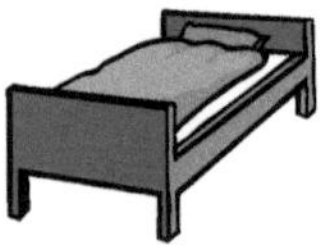

침대

bed

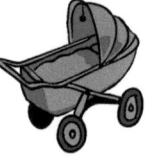

유모차

stroller

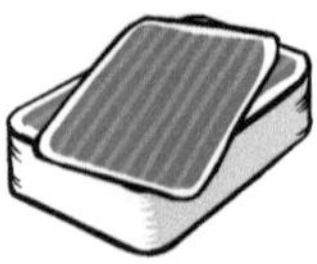

카드 게임

deck of cards

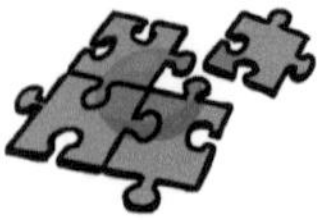

퍼즐

jigsaw

SUPER
MEGA

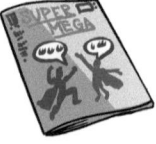

만화

comic

레고

lego bricks

장난감 블럭

toy blocks

액션 캐릭터

action figure

베이비 그로

romper suit

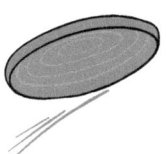

프리스비

frisbee

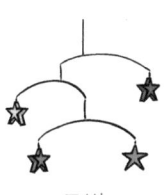

모빌

mobile

보드 게임

board game

주사위

dice

기차 모형 세트

model train set

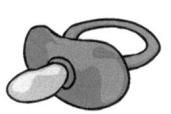

노리개 젖꼭지

pacifier

파티

party

그림책

picture book

공

ball

인형

doll

놀다

play

모래상자

sandpit

그네

swing

장난감

toys

비디오 게임 콘솔

video game console

세바퀴자전거

tricycle

곰인형

teddy bear

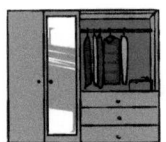

옷장

wardrobe

의복

clothing

양말

socks

스타킹

stockings

스타킹

tights

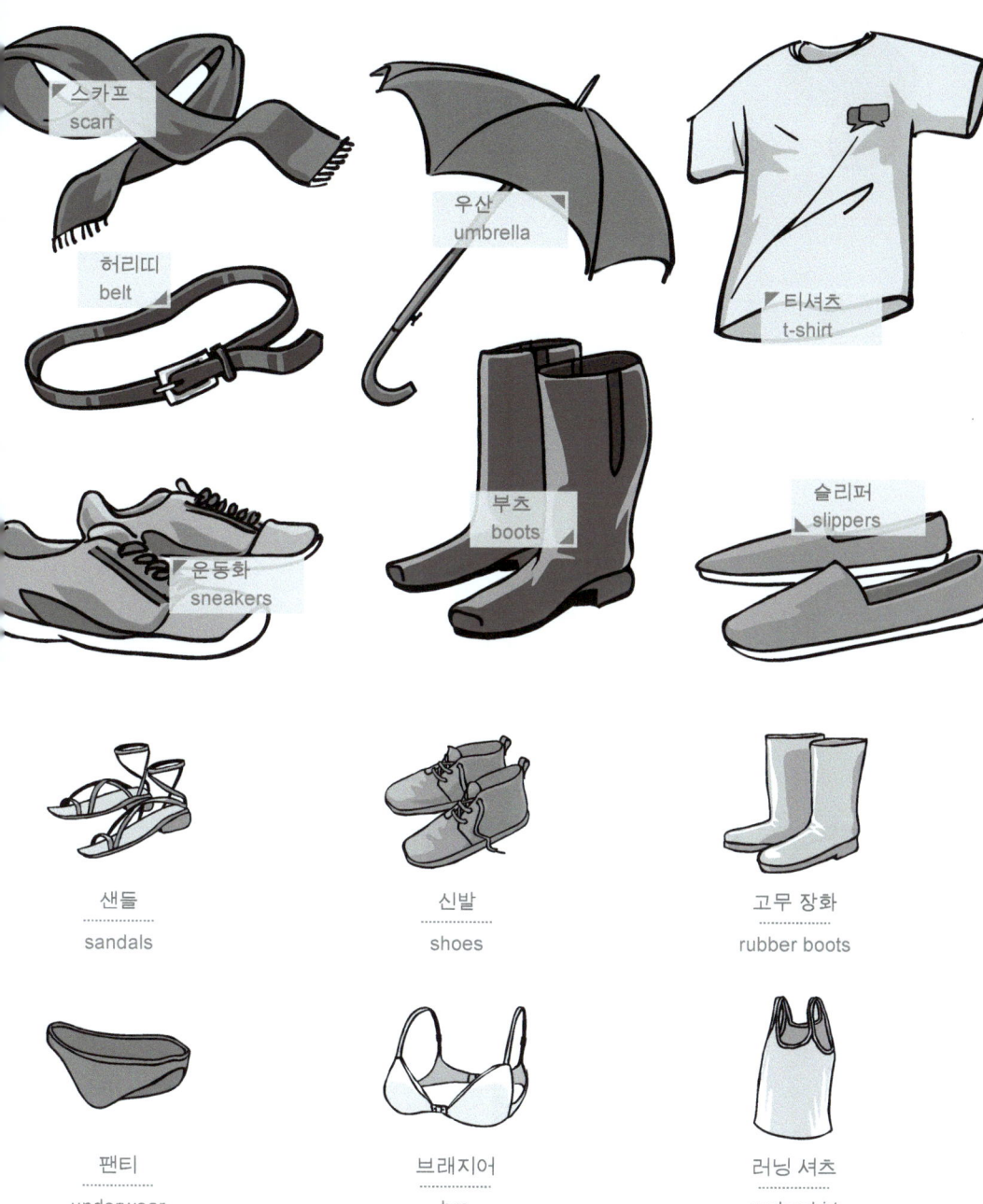

스카프
scarf

우산
umbrella

티셔츠
t-shirt

허리띠
belt

부츠
boots

슬리퍼
slippers

운동화
sneakers

샌들
sandals

신발
shoes

고무 장화
rubber boots

팬티
underwear

브래지어
bra

러닝 셔츠
undershirt

바디

body

바지

pants

청바지

jeans

치마

skirt

블라우스

blouse

셔츠

shirt

폴오버

pullover

후드티

sweater

블레이저

blazer

자켓

jacket

외투

coat

비옷

raincoat

의상

costume

원피스

dress

웨딩 드레스

wedding dress

양복

suit

나이트가운

nightgown

잠옷

pajamas

사리

sari

두건

headscarf

터번

turban

부르카

burka

카프탄

kaftan

아바야

abaya

수영복

swimsuit

수영바지

trunks

반바지

shorts

트레이닝복

tracksuit

앞치마

apron

장갑

gloves

단추

button

안경

glasses

팔찌

bracelet

목걸이

necklace

반지

ring

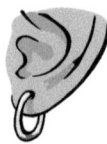

귀걸이

earring

캡 모자

cap

옷걸이

coat hanger

모자

hat

넥타이

tie

지퍼

zip

헬멧

helmet

멜빵

braces

교복

school uniform

유니폼

uniform

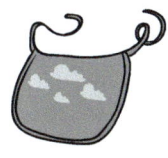

턱받이

bib

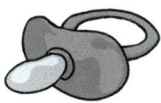

노리개 젖꼭지

pacifier

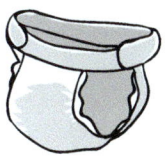

기저귀

diaper

사무실
office

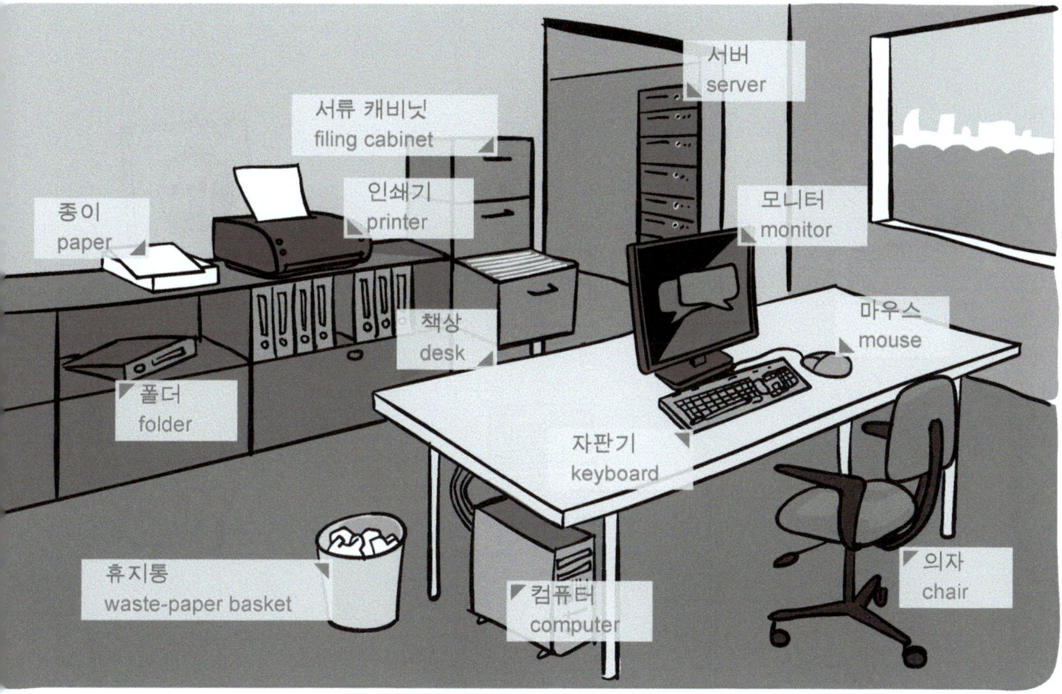
서버
server
서류 캐비닛
filing cabinet
인쇄기
printer
종이
paper
모니터
monitor
책상
desk
마우스
mouse
폴더
folder
자판기
keyboard
휴지통
waste-paper basket
컴퓨터
computer
의자
chair

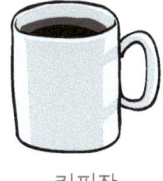

커피잔

coffee mug

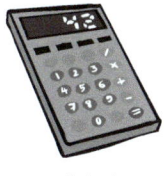

계산기

calculator

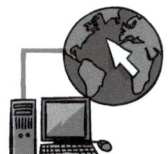

인터넷

internet

노트북

laptop

편지

letter

메시지

message

휴대전화

cell phone

네트워크

network

복사기

photocopier

소프트웨어

software

전화

telephone

플러그 소켓

plug socket

팩시밀리

fax machine

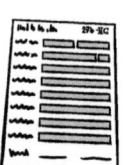

서식

form

서류

document

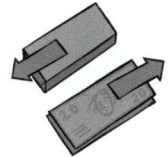

사다

buy

지불하다

pay

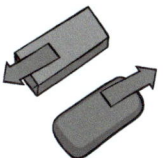

거래하다

trade

돈

money

달러

dollar

유로

euro

엔

yen

루블

rouble

스위스 프랑

Swiss franc

위안

renminbi yuan

루피

rupee

현금인출기

cash point

환전소

currency exchange office

금

gold

은

silver

석유

oil

에너지

energy

가격

price

계약

contract

세금

tax

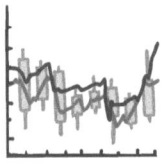

주식

stock

일하다

work

근로자

employee

고용주

employer

공장

factory

상점

shop

직업
occupations

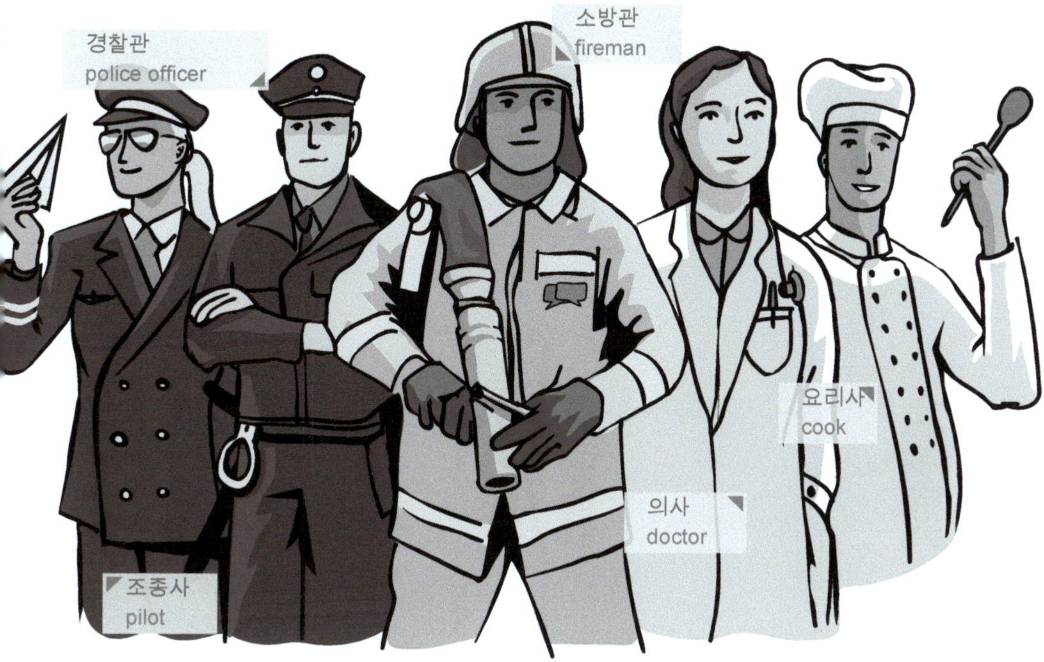

경찰관
police officer
소방관
fireman
요리사
cook
의사
doctor
조종사
pilot

정원사

gardener

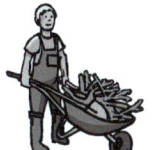

목수

carpenter

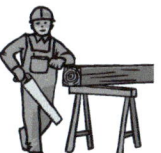

수선공

seamstress

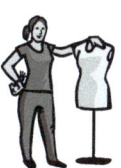

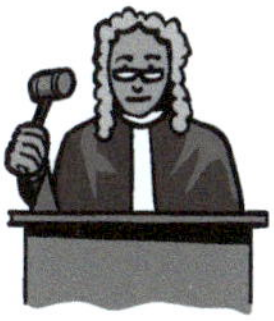

판사

judge

화학자

chemist

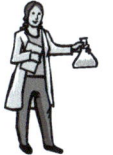

배우

actor

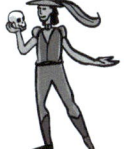

버스운전사

bus driver

택시 운전사

taxi driver

어부

fisherman

청소부

cleaning lady

지붕 수리자

roofer

웨이터

waiter

사냥꾼

hunter

화가

painter

제빵사

baker

전기업자

electrician

건축업자

builder

엔지니어

engineer

정육점업자

butcher

배관업자

plumber

우편물 배달부

postman

군인

soldier

건축가

architect

계산원

cashier

플로리스트

florist

미용사

hairdresser

검표원

conductor

정비사

mechanic

선장

captain

치과의사

dentist

학자

scientist

유대교 라비

rabbi

이맘

imam

수도승

monk

사제

pastor

tools

망치
hammer

펜치
pliers

나사 드라이버
screwdriver

렌치
wrench

손전등
torch

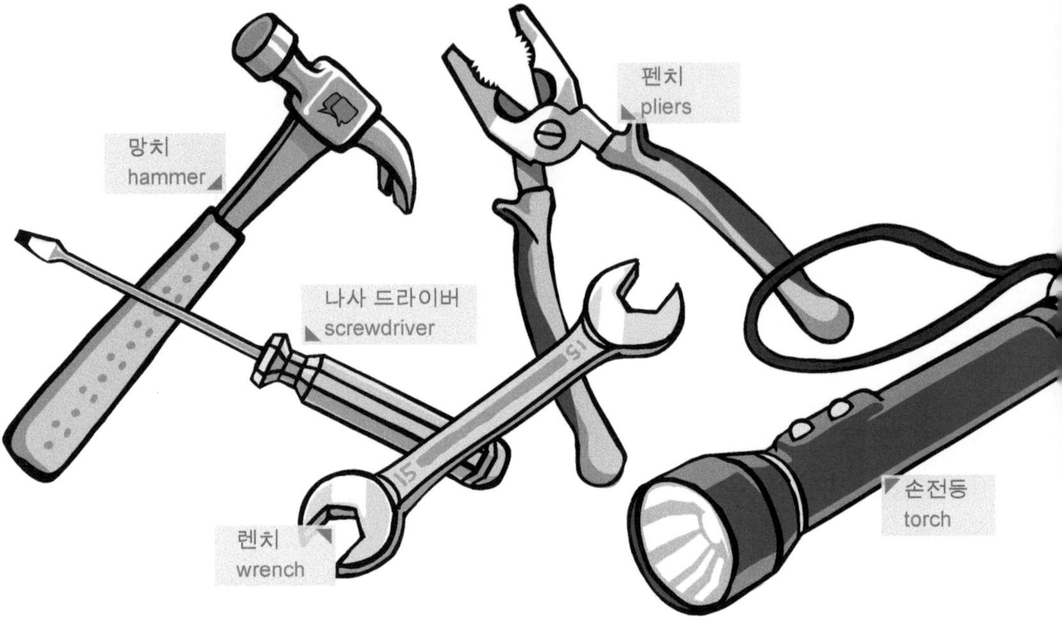

굴삭기

excavator

연장통

toolbox

사다리

ladder

톱

saw

못

nails

드릴

drill

수리하다
repair

삽
shovel

젠장!
Damn!

쓰레받기
dustpan

페인트통
paint can

나사
screws

악기

musical instruments

스피커
loud speaker

드럼
drum set

기타
guitar

콘트라베이스
double bass

트럼펫
trumpet

피아노

piano

바이올린

violin

베이스

bass

팀파니

timpani

북

drums

키보드

keyboard

색소폰

saxophone

플루트

flute

마이크

microphone

동물원

ZOO

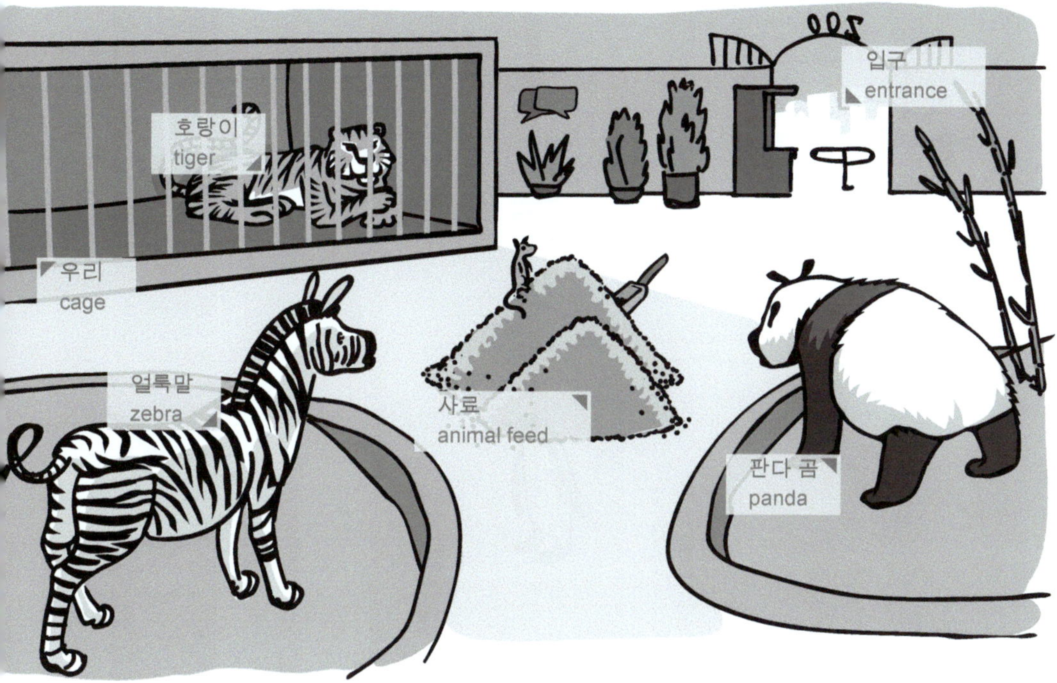

입구
entrance
호랑이
tiger
우리
cage
얼룩말
zebra
사료
animal feed
판다 곰
panda

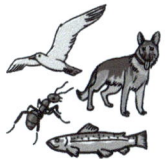

동물

animals

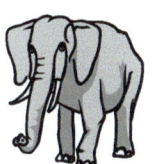

코끼리

elephant

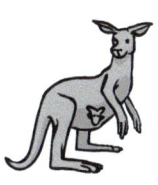

캥거루

kangaroo

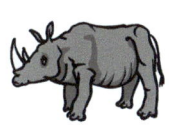

코뿔소

rhino

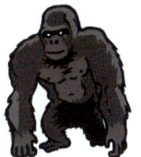

고릴라

gorilla

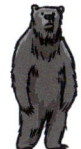

곰

bear

낙타
camel

타조
ostrich

사자
lion

원숭이
monkey

홍학
flamingo

앵무새
parrot

북극곰
polar bear

펭귄
penguin

상어
shark

공작
peacock

뱀
snake

악어
crocodile

동물원 사육사
zookeeper

물개
seal

재규어
jaguar

조랑말

pony

표범

leopard

하마

hippo

기린

giraffe

독수리

eagle

맷돼지

boar

생선

fish

거북이

turtle

바다코끼리

walrus

여우

fox

영양

gazelle

미식축구
American football

자전거 경기
cycling

테니스
tennis

농구
basketball

수영
swimming

권투
boxing

아이스하키
ice hockey

축구

soccer

배드민턴

badminton

육상 경기

athletics

핸드볼

handball

스키

skiing

폴로

polo

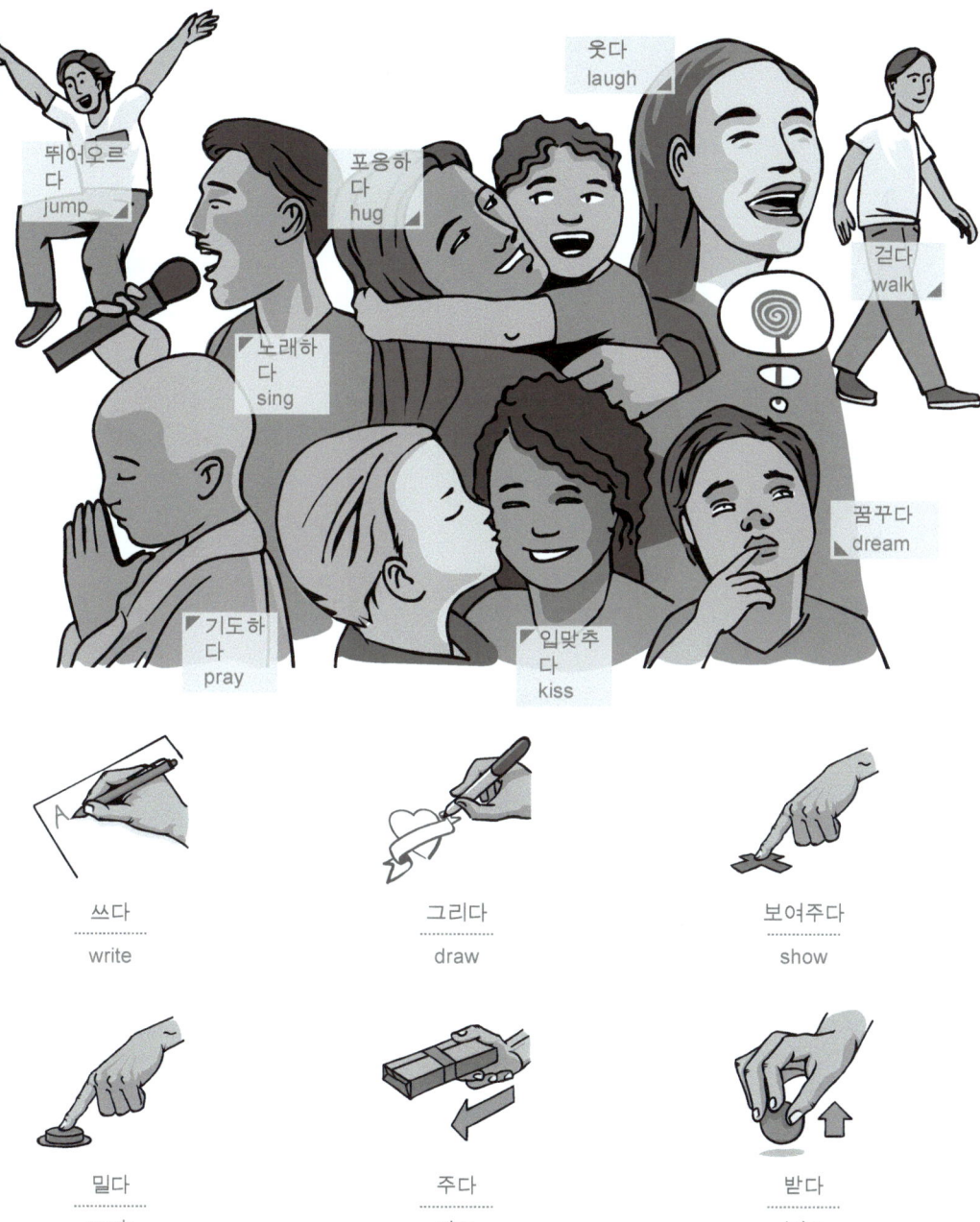

뛰어오르다
jump

포옹하다
hug

옷다
laugh

걷다
walk

노래하다
sing

꿈꾸다
dream

기도하다
pray

입맞추다
kiss

쓰다
write

그리다
draw

보여주다
show

밀다
push

주다
give

받다
take

가지다

have

행하다

do

...이다

be

서있다

stand

뛰다

run

당기다

pull

던지다

throw

떨어지다

fall

누워있다

lie

기다리다

wait

운반하다

carry

앉다

sit

옷을 입다

get dressed

자다

sleep

깨다

wake up

보다

look at

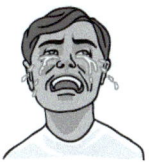

울다

cry

쓰다듬다

stroke

빗다

comb

말하다

talk

이해하다

understand

묻다

ask

듣다

listen

마시다

drink

먹다

eat

정리하다

tidy up

사랑하다

love

요리하다

cook

주행하다

drive

날다

fly

활동 - activities

해항하다

sail

계산하다

calculate

읽다

read

배우다

learn

일하다

work

결혼하다

marry

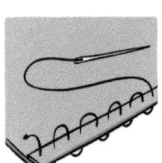

바느질하다

sew

이를 닦다

brush teeth

죽이다

kill

담배 피우다

smoke

보내다

send

가족

family

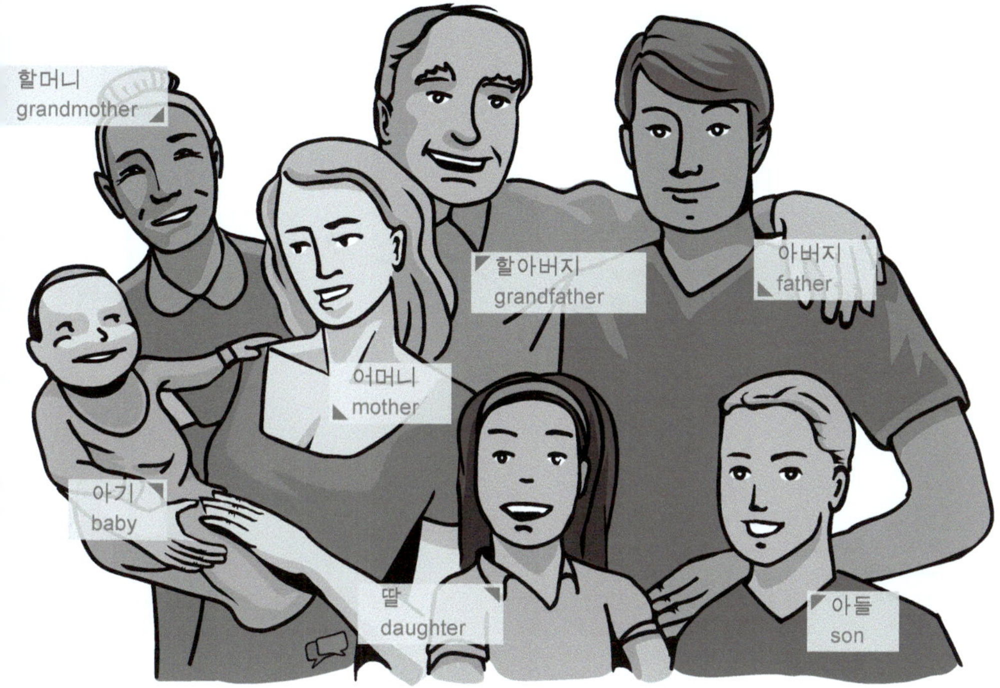
할머니
grandmother
할아버지
grandfather
아버지
father
어머니
mother
아기
baby
딸
daughter
아들
son

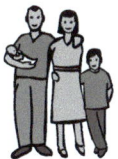

손님

guest

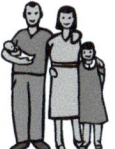

이모 / 고모

aunt

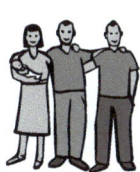

삼촌

uncle

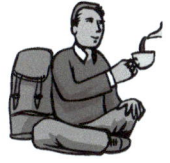

형제

brother

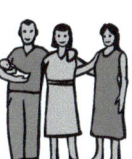

자매

sister

몸통

body

이마
forehead
눈
eye
어깨
shoulder
손가락
finger
얼굴
face
턱
chin
손가락
hand
다리
leg
가슴
breast
팔
arm

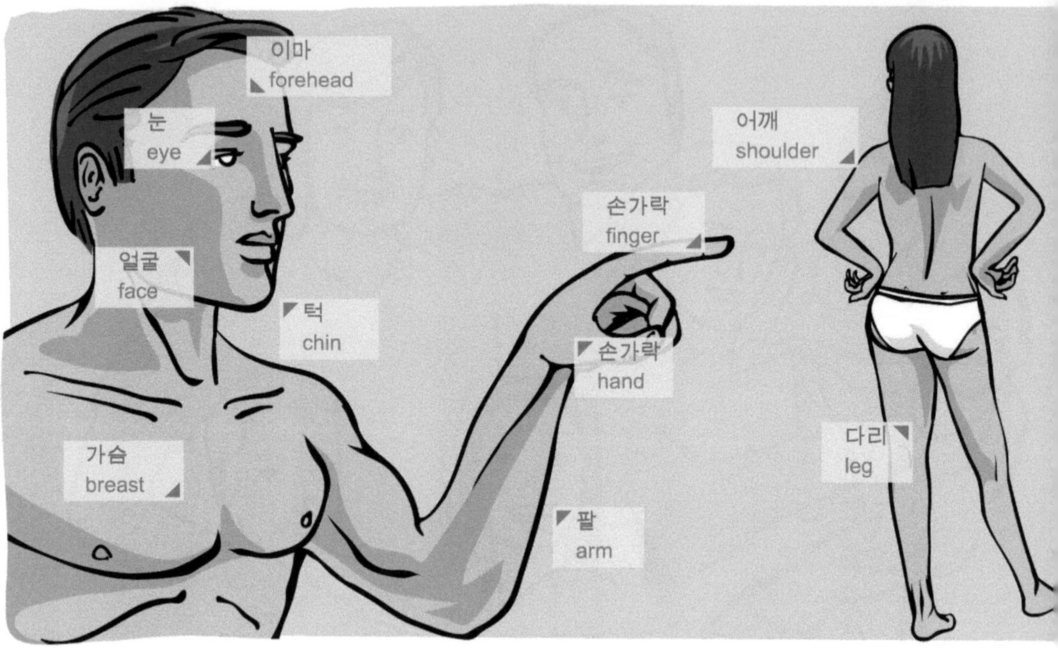

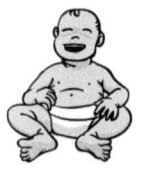

아기

baby

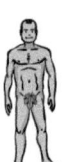

남자

man

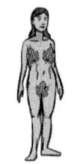

여자

woman

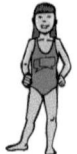

소녀

girl

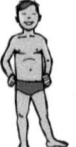

소년

boy

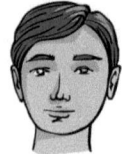

머리카락

head

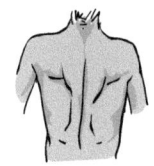

등
back

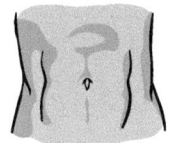

배
belly

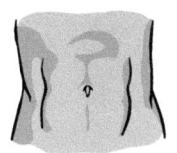

배꼽
navel

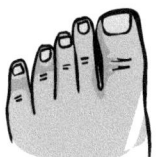

발가락
toe

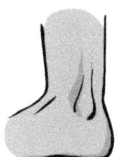

발꿈치
heel

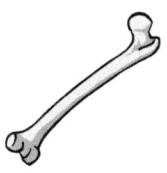

뼈
bone

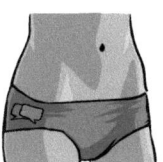

엉덩이
hip

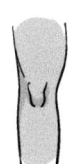

무릎
knee

팔꿈치
elbow

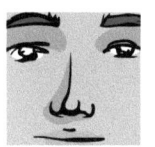

코
nose

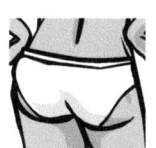

둔부
buttocks

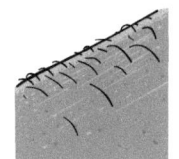

피부
skin

뺨
cheek

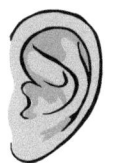

귀
ear

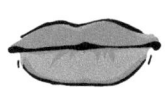

입술
lip

몸통 - body

입
mouth

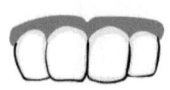

치아
tooth

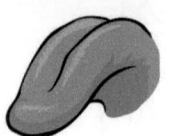

혀
tongue

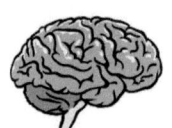

뇌
brain

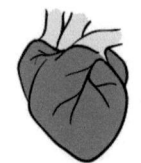

심장
heart

근육
muscle

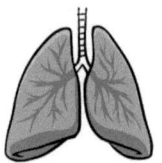

허파
lung

간
liver

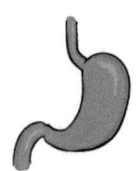

위
stomach

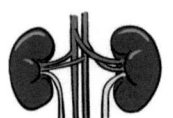

신장
kidneys

성교
sex

콘돔
condom

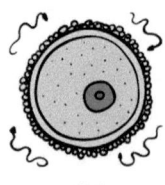

난자
ovum

정자
semen

임신
pregnancy

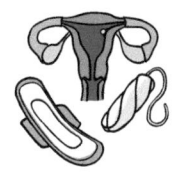

월경

menstruation

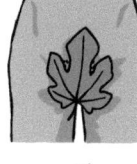

질

vagina

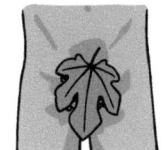

음경

penis

눈썹

eyebrow

머리카락

hair

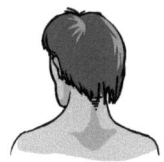

목

neck

병원
hospital

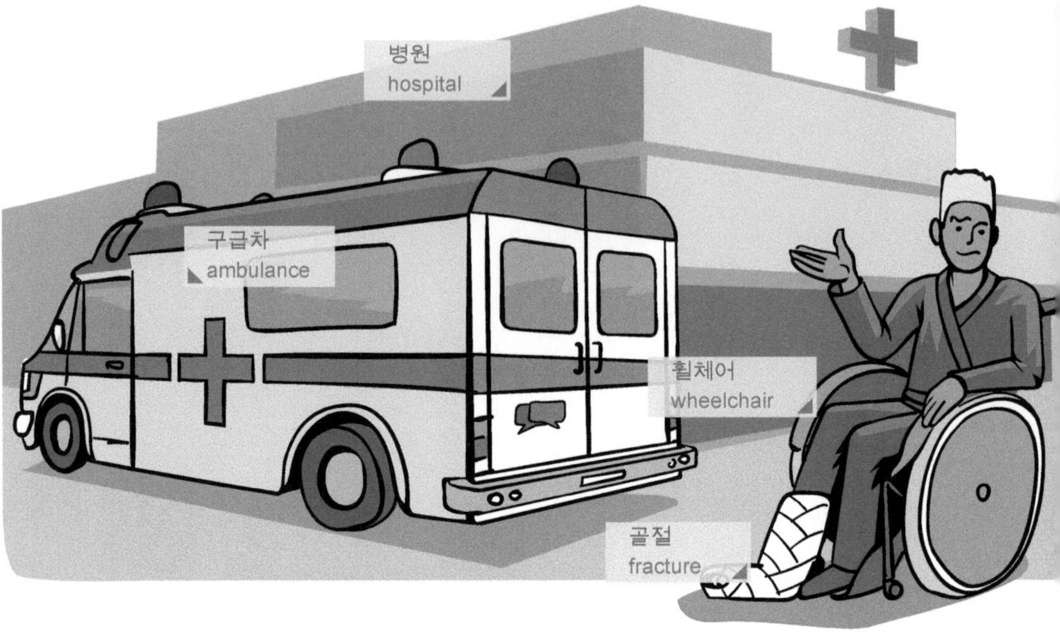

병원
hospital
구급차
ambulance
휠체어
wheelchair
골절
fracture

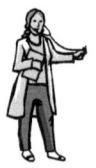

의사

doctor

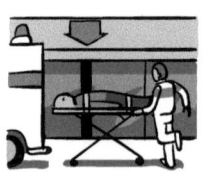

응급실

emergency room

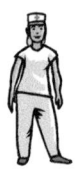

간호사

nurse

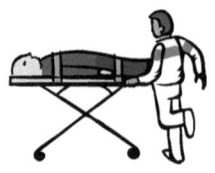

응급상황

emergency

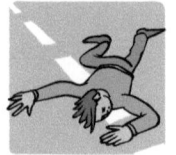

혼수상태

unconscious

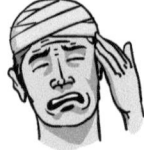

통증

pain

부상

injury

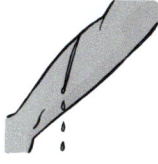

출혈

bleeding

심장마비

heart attack

뇌졸증

stroke

알러지

allergy

기침

cough

열

fever

독감

flu

설사

diarrhea

두통

headache

암

cancer

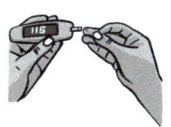

당뇨병

diabetes

외과의

surgeon

수술용 메스

scalpel

수술

operation

CT
CT

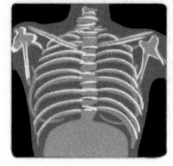

엑스레이
x-ray

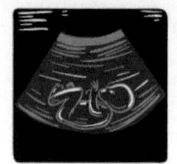

초음파
ultrasound

마스크
face mask

질병
disease

대기실
waiting room

목발
crutch

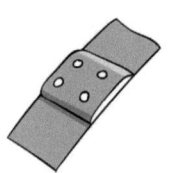

반창고
plaster

붕대
bandage

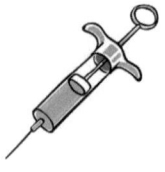

주사
injection

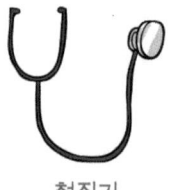

청진기
stethoscope

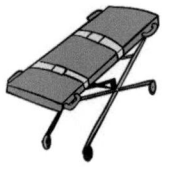

들것
stretcher

체온계
clinical thermometer

출생
birth

과체중
overweight

보청기

hearing aid

소독약

disinfectant

감염

infection

바이러스

virus

HIV / AIDS

HIV / AIDS

의학

medicine

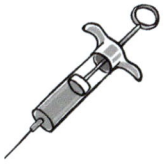

예방접종

vaccination

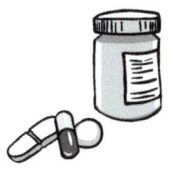

알약

tablets

알약

pill

구급 전화

emergency call

혈압측정기

blood pressure monitor

병든 / 건강한

ill / healthy

도와주세요!

Help!

경보음

alarm

폭행

assault

공격

attack

위험

danger

비상구

emergency exit

불이야!

Fire!

소화기

fire extinguisher

사고

accident

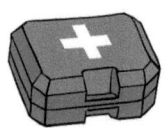

구급 상자

first-aid kit

SOS

SOS

경찰

police

유럽

Europe

북미

North America

남미

South America

아프리카

Africa

아시아

Asia

호주

Australia

북극

Atlantic

태평양

Pacific

인도양

Indian Ocean

남극해

Antarctic Ocean

북극해

Arctic Ocean

북극해

North pole

남극해

South pole

남극

Antarctica

지구

earth

육지

land

바다

sea

섬

island

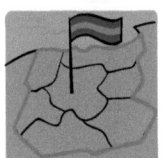

국가

nation

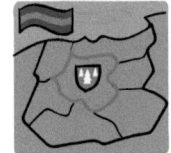

주

state

시계 문자판

clock face

시침

hour hand

분침

minute hand

초침

second hand

몇 시입니까?

What time is it?

일

day

시간

time

지금

now

디지털 시계

digital watch

분

minute

시간

hour

주간

week

월요일
Monday

수요일
Wednesday

금요일
Friday

화요일
Tuesday

목요일
Thursday

토요일
Saturday

일요일
Sunday

어제
yesterday

오늘
today

내일
tomorrow

아침
morning

정오
noon

저녁
evening

근로일
workdays

주말
weekend

비
▶ rain

무지개
▶ rainbow

바람
▶ wind

눈
▶ snow

봄
▶ spring

여름
summer

가을
fall

겨울
winter

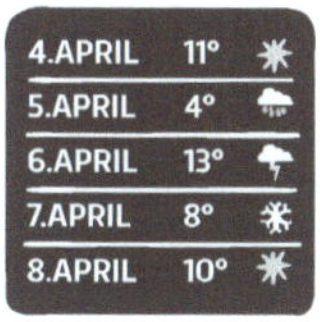

4.APRIL	11°	☀
5.APRIL	4°	☁
6.APRIL	13°	☁
7.APRIL	8°	❅
8.APRIL	10°	☀

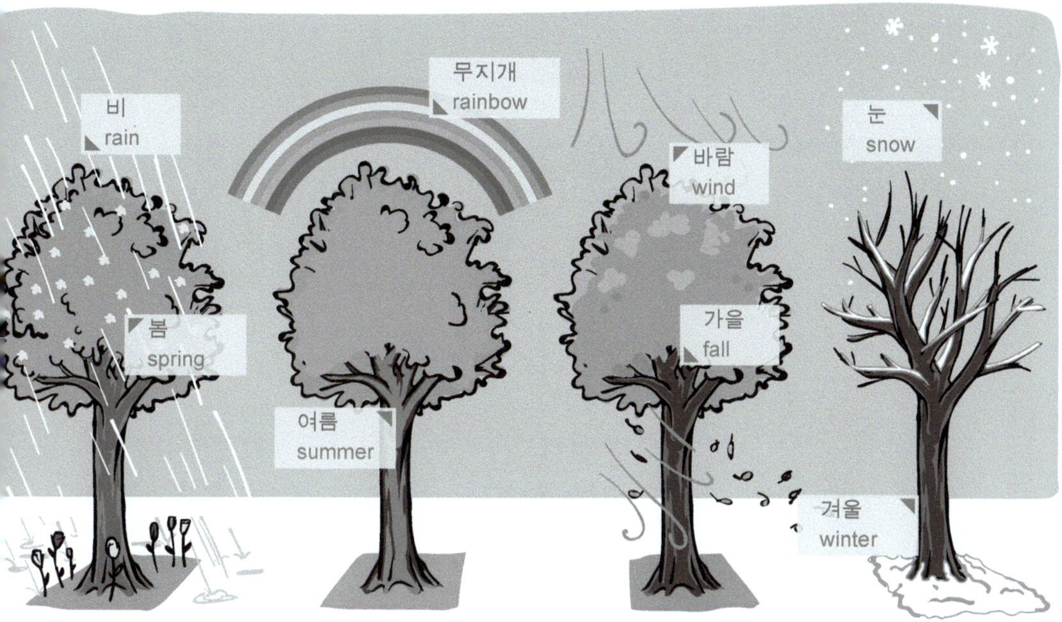

날씨 예보
weather forecast

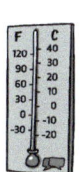

온도계
thermometer

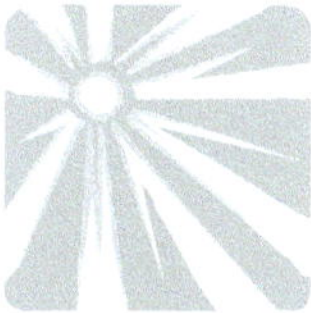

햇빛
sunshine

구름
cloud

안개
fog

습도
humidity

번개

lightning

천둥

thunder

폭풍

storm

우박

hail

장마

monsoon

홍수

flood

얼음

ice

1월

January

2월

February

3월

March

4월

April

5월

May

6월

June

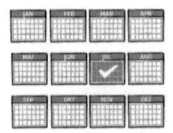

7월

July

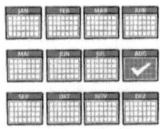

8월

August

년도 - year

9월

September

10월

October

11월

November

12월

December

형태

shapes

원

circle

정사각형

square

직사각형

rectangle

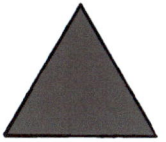

삼각형

triangle

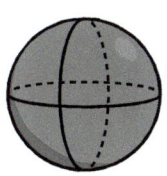

구

sphere

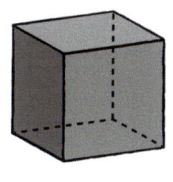

정사면체

cube

하양

white

노랑

yellow

주황

orange

분홍

pink

빨강

red

보라

purple

파랑

blue

초록

green

갈색

brown

회색

gray

검정

black

많은 / 적은

a lot / a little

화난 / 차분한

angry / calm

아름다운 / 추한

beautiful / ugly

시작 / 끝

beginning / end

큰 / 작은

big / small

밝은 / 어두운

bright / dark

형제 / 자매

brother / sister

깨끗한 / 더러운

clean / dirty

완전한 / 불완전한

complete / incomplete

낮 / 밤

day / night

죽은 / 산

dead / alive

넓은 / 좁은

wide / narrow

삭용의 / 비식용의

edible / inedible

불친절한 / 친절한

evil / kind

흥분된 / 지루한

excited / bored

뚱뚱한 / 마른

fat / thin

처음으로 / 마지막으로

first / last

친구 / 적

friend / enemy

꽉 찬 / 텅 빈

full / empty

딱딱한 / 부드러운

hard / soft

무거운 / 가벼운

heavy / light

배고픔 / 목마름

hunger / thirst

병든 / 건강한

ill / healthy

불법 / 합법

illegal / legal

영리한 / 어리석은

intelligent / stupid

왼 / 오른

left / right

가까운 / 먼

near / far

새 / 헌

new / used

무 / 유

nothing / something

늙은 / 젊은

old / young

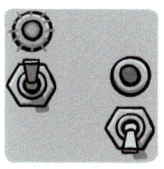

온 / 오프

on / off

열린 / 닫힌

open / closed

조용한 / 시끄러운

quiet / loud

부유한 / 가난한

rich / poor

옳은 / 틀린

right / wrong

거친 / 매끄러운

rough / smooth

슬픈 / 기쁜

sad / happy

짧은 / 긴

short / long

느린 / 빠른

slow / fast

젖은 / 마른

wet / dry

따뜻한 / 시원한

warm / cool

전쟁 / 평화

war / peace

반대 - opposites

0

영

zero

1

하나

one

2

둘

two

3

셋

three

4

넷

four

5

다섯

five

6

여섯

six

7

일곱

seven

8

여덟

eight

9

아홉

nine

10

열

ten

11

열하나

eleven

12
열둘

twelve

13
열셋

thirteen

14
열넷

fourteen

15
열다섯

fifteen

16
열여섯

sixteen

17
열일곱

seventeen

18
열여덟

eighteen

19
열아홉

nineteen

20
스물

twenty

100
백

hundred

1.000
천

thousand

1.000.000
백만

million

영어

English

미국식 영어

American English

중국어 만다린

Chinese Mandarin

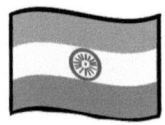

힌두어

Hindi

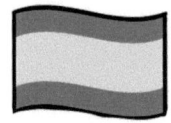

스페인어

Spanish

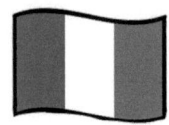

프랑스어

French

아랍어

Arabic

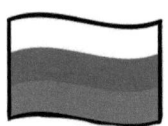

러시아어

Russian

포르투갈어

Portuguese

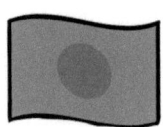

불가리아어

Bengali

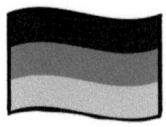

독일어

German

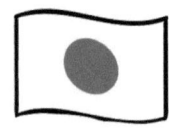

일본어

Japanese

나
I

너
you

그 / 그녀/ 그것
he / she / it

우리
we

너희들
you

그들
they

누가?
who?

무엇이?
what?

어떻게?
how?

어디서?
where?

언제?
when?

HELLO, I AM

이름
name

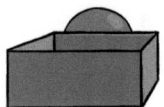

뒤에

behind

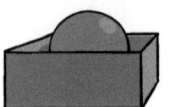

안에

in

앞에

in front of

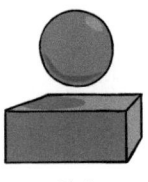

위에

over

위에

on

아래에

under

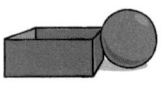

옆에

beside

사이에

between

장소

place